# HOW TO AVOID COMMON PITFALLS IN MARRIAGE

Johnson Manuel Adams

Table of Content

# INTRODUCTION

Indeed, even relationships that seem, by all accounts, to be awesome, will have marriage issues.

Having issues in marriage isn't the most concerning issue.

The most concerning issue isn't knowing how to impart through these issues with the goal you finding the arrangement.

Unfortunately, marriage correspondence is the main driver of numerous conjugal issues.

To this end, I suggest pre-marriage mentoring.

Mentoring frequently gives the specialized instruments couples need to have a solid marriage.

Assuming your marriage has issues on this rundown, that are not being dealt with predictably, then your marriage might be in a tough situation.

Figure out how to explore and conquer the obstacles introduced by normal marriage issues, beginning with this fundamental asset.

Nonetheless, here is a thorough rundown that you ought to truly study. Concentrate on this rundown to get familiar with the normal reasons for marriage issues looked by wedded couples, and figure out how to reliably apply the arrangements advertised.

Doing so will guarantee that issues in your marriage don't ultimately prompt separation. The objective isn't figuring out how to, never have marriage issues.

The objective is to figure out how to rapidly and obviously distinguish your marriage issues.

Once distinguished, figure out how to decently and consciously resolve them.

Remember that numerous issues in marriage.

# 11 NORMAL MIX-UPS WEDDED COUPLES MAKE THAT YOU WANT TO STAY AWAY FROM

Individuals commit errors, that is typical. However, a few deficiencies or false impressions can seriously endanger your relationship in the event that you do it continually and in long haul, particularly as a wedded couple. We're not saying that you shouldn't commit any error whatsoever, however by monitoring the normal mistakes that you or your future mate possibly make in your forthcoming marriage, you'll gain from it and improve. All things considered, planning counteraction is superior to a fix, right? Thus, ensure you understand what sort of conduct that you ought to keep away from as portrayed beneath:

# 1. Raising past issues

Once in a while attempting to determine recent, two or three moves their concentration to past issues all things considered. Perhaps they're actually holding resentment or feel like the new issue originated from old unfortunate behavior patterns. One way or the other, doing this will just put forward your viewpoints ineffectual and unconstructive, particularly assuming both of them has concurred that the previous issues are as of now settled. Put your consideration regarding the issue you confronted today, figure out how to continue on, and don't drag past conflicts into the new condition. Like that, you can try not to quarrel over a similar stuff again and again from here on out.

## 2. Not keeping up with closeness

This mix-up normally made unwittingly, particularly by wedded couples who have been hitched for a long while or getting more occupied every day with works or children. At the point when there are an excessive number of interruptions around you, it's not difficult to want to be personal is presently not a need. Subsequently, the couple became far off, disengaged, and floating separated from one another. Regardless of how occupied or focused on you are with day to day existence, or how long you've been hitched, keep up with the closeness among you and your mate. Beside engaging in sexual relations, you can likewise design a standard night out or reliably giving each other little yet sweet actual signals, similar to a kiss prior to leaving the house or a genuine, profound embrace to show the amount you missed them toward the finish of a drawn out day.

## 3. Permitting others to get too engaged with the relationship

At times, a wedded couple's marriage isn't only including the spouse and the wife, yet in addition the guardians, parents in law, even dearest companions, chief, or others outside their inward circle. It's unquestionably good to have a strong and solid emotionally supportive network to help you and your mate while you're dealing with a specific issue. Yet, in the event that those individuals ended up being controlling, constantly hovering over or making things more convoluted, then hopefully it's not past the time to switch things up. In this way, before you incorporate pointless gatherings into your relationship, recall that you and your life partner need to define limits in regards to outside contribution, for instance by not enlightening others concerning the unseen struggles in your marriage. Since what significant is the way you two need to depend on one another to endure this drawn out venture.

## 4. Anticipating that the companion should guess what you might be thinking

This point sort of makes sense of why correspondence is the way in to an effective marriage. Now and again, wedded couples feel like they have known one another alright so their companion ought to understand what they feel or need without talking about it without holding back. Yet, when the companion neglected to do as such, they would feel incredibly disheartened. Truth be told, your companion isn't telepathic, as are you. While it's charming to realize that he can get you some espresso before you ask, that wouldn't generally be the situation. Particularly in a more perplexing setting, similar to the justification for why you gave him a quiet treatment after a battle or how you wish he truly focuses on you. Continuously attempt to convey your interests, wants, wishes, and assumptions plainly, it'll save investment likewise assist you with finding the arrangements all the more productively.

## 5. Battling to win

All couples battle, yet some do it to track down goals, and some basically need to vent out the indignation and dissatisfactions toward one another. Some do it far more atrocious; they contend to demonstrate that they're in every case right and keeping the score between one another; who's on the right track in the last contention, who's the washout and who wins this time. At the point when you're hitched, always remember that you're in the same boat with your companion. Along these lines, his misfortune is yours too, as well as the other way around. Consider all the battling and contending to be an opportunity to think twice about clear up any question among you.

## 6. Bringing a kid into a disturbed marriage

It's miserable yet obvious; several sees having a child as an exit plan and answer for their upset marriage. Truly, you shouldn't put such a major liability of carrying a family harmony to a guiltless kid. Beside that, all of the pressure of having another child, hormonal swings, even post pregnancy anxiety can compound the situation and make new issues for the unexperienced parents. The kids will likewise possibly grow up watching their folks battling all time, which is another parental mix-up a couple ought to keep away from. Taking a stab at tackling the difficulties among you and your life partner prior to choosing to extend your family would be savvier. With a solid and better-created connection among you and your companion, you can give your kids a superior climate to grow up.

## 7. Not discussing sex enough

As connecting with the closeness point, some couple likewise skipped having a legitimate measure of essential sex talk with one another. Why discuss it when you can get it done, you could inquire. Indeed, this is on the grounds that having intercourse is far beyond carrying out the things. You really want to communicate your needs and wants to one another plainly, as well as your abhorrences, dread, or dreams with the goal that you two genuinely partake in each close second, be in total agreement about it, and don't feel like you're passing up something in your sexual coexistence. So don't be timid or reluctant to discuss it, you can figure out how to join or think twice about your life partner's inclinations, or you can figure out different things to investigate together as you got more insight and need to keep the flash alive following a couple of long periods of marriage.

## 8. Not being open about finance

Another misstep that most hitched couples make isn't overall completely open to one another about their monetary circumstance or issues. The wife could conceal the receipts from her lavish shopping trips, or the husband contributed a major piece of their cash into an endeavor without telling his life partner. Realizing that cash issue is one of the principal reasons in separate, we can't pressure that it is so vital to be straightforward and fair with one another with regards to the subject of family finance. A couple ought to know precisely how much cash they are making, spending, money management, owing, loaning, or getting. Keeping an escape clause about this will just prompt difficulty, sometime. Thus, attempt to consistently discuss your financial issue and ideally you can continuously tackle it or arrive at a shared objective together.

# 9. Disregarding issues that should be settled

Regardless of how little, a wedded couple shouldn't hide an issue away from plain view and disregard it. Since when they do, generally it just develops into a more concerning issue that would ultimately be more diligently to deal with. Thus, as a prospective wedded couple or love birds, ensure you make the propensity for taking care of an issue when it emerges. It's alright assuming it requires investment to track down the arrangement, however remember, keep away from, or disregard it through and through.

# 10. Settle on choice without speaking with one another

Being in a group with your mate implies that you ought to continuously consider their perspective while settling on a choice, particularly ones in regards to the family, cash, vocation, or other significant life bearing. However, actually, loads of hitched couples commit the error of not counseling their companion while arranging or settling on things. Perhaps they are still prone to live freely as a solitary, yet that thing ought to change the second you said I do. To make the change more straightforward, attempt to begin including your future companion in your likely arrangements and objectives, so you can likewise place their thoughts and decisions into thought. That's what by doing, when you're hitched, you wouldn't cause each other to understand left or unheard.

## 11. Underestimating one another

One of the most terrible mix-up a wedded couple could make is underestimating one another. Not offering your thanks and appreciation toward each other is one thing to make it happen. Be that as it may, a few couples basically don't give sufficient time for their significant other or spouse, such as getting occupied by work or screens constantly. While, as a matter of fact, time is the most valuable thing you can provide for your friends and family. Try not to misstep the same way as these sorts of couples. Right from the start as far as possible, ensure your companion generally feels cherished, appreciated, and worth your consistently. The words 'thank you' and 'I love you' are known to have an enchanted impact when said genuinely and ceaselessly, likewise put forth the attempt to have some quality time with one another to revive the warmth and support your relationship

## TYPICAL PITFALLS OF MARRIAGE TO STAY AWAY FROM

No couple sets out on wedded life hoping to wind up in separate from court. However, that is what befalls more than 1,000,000 American couples every year. What's more, when they do the posthumous, they frequently find their marriage was subverted by one of these 10 snares:

## 1. Underestimating your accomplice.

That resembles having a nursery that you're not weeding or treating, says an expert, teacher of human turn of events and family learns at Indiana

College. "You can't guess that it ought to continue to prosper."

Let your accomplice in on you value the person in question.

## 2. Failing to remember that a decent marriage takes work.

"Individuals believe that having a blissful marriage is an enchanted, mysterious event," says marriage and family specialist Dr. Leslie Parrott. He is the co-creator of When Terrible Things Happen to Great Relationships (Zondervan/HarperCollins). "We've recognized the way that supporting takes a lot of skill.

 However, we would rather not acknowledge the possibility that heartfelt love takes a lot of work, as well."

## 3. Not talking through struggle.

Assuming you depend on weighty murmurs, hammered entryways and other non-verbal correspondence when something is annoying you,

you could be behaving recklessly. As difficult as it could be to kick the discussion off, you should shout out. "In any case, issues begin rotting and start to take on a unique kind of energy," makes sense of Sharon Naylor, creator of The Informal Manual for Separation (Hungry Personalities).

## 4. Neglecting to sentiment your accomplice.

We as a whole need to be caused to feel unique. "That is the reason it's so essential to save not less than one night of the week for yourself as well as your companion. Utilize this ordinary 'night out' to share your deepest desires."

## 5. Battling grimy.

The better you know someone, the more straightforward it is to harmed that individual. "Despite how furious you may be connected to something."

"You really want to oppose the impulse to sort out the one thing that will hurt your accomplice the most and afterward utilize that against him."

## 6. Battling about cash.

A new report in large numbers Dollar Round Table, a global relationship of extra security and monetary administrations experts, viewed that as 43% of hitched couples quarrel over cash. In the event that cash's turning into a significant wellspring of contention, you should seriously mull over plunking down with a monetary organizer or some other outsider that can help concoct a monetary blueprint you both can live with.

## 7. Allowing the energy to fail.

"Have intercourse frequently. Whenever both of you is in that frame of mind." "Assuming you hold on until the two accomplices are in that frame of mind, you won't wind up having a lot of sex by any means. Also, over the long run, you'll wind up floating separated."

## 8. Closing down physically when you're furious instead of managing issues.

In spite of the fact that keeping warmth might seem like the best method for rebuffing your accomplice, you risk genuinely harming your relationship.

## 9. Neglecting to comprehend that relationships have high points and low points.

"Expecting to astound minutes in your marriage is okay." "Simply don't anticipate that they should happen consistently."

## 10. Tapping out too without any problem.

"We're so familiar with the idea of out of date quality that we treat our accomplices as expendable." He is a Chicago separate from lawyer and creator. Commitment to revive the blazes as opposed to searching for the nearest get away from hatch.

# 7 Things That Can Obliterate a Marriage or Long haul Relationship, and How to Keep away from Them

It's a platitude that the most concerning issues in marriage spin around cash and sex — yet these aren't the main regions that can represent the deciding moment a drawn out relationship. A large group of unfortunate elements, harmful ways of behaving, and unfortunate needs can mean the distinction among flourishing and coming up short.

There are four harbingers of despondent relationships he calls the Four Horsemen. "These incorporate analysis, disdain, stalling, and preventiveness."These are approaches to acting demonstrated in relationship components that are demonstrated to hurt after some time."

To keep up with solid, blissful close connections, it's critical to detect (and root out) normal issues that can prompt disagreement or even separation. Somehow, a significant number of the things that obliterate marriage are established in the purported Four Horsemen. In any case, others go past this rubric. Little, regular struggles can amount to conjugal difficulty, or some of the time further issues show up to wreak havoc.

Here is a glance at seven normal ways of behaving that can obliterate a marriage or long haul relationship — and how to fix them before they do.

# 1. You Convey Ineffectively or Not the least bit

Nobody will be astonished to discover that unfortunate correspondence debases connections. On the off chance that one or the two individuals from a couple feel unheard, put down, or shut out, building a connection is troublesome in the event that certainly feasible.

Unfortunate correspondence includes many appearances inside marriage. Now and again, it can seem to be a powerlessness to consult with your life partner about how you're truly feeling. This can ultimately prompt unstable feelings. **"Without having the choice to impart opinions reliably, little issues change into covered, stifled sentiments that air pocket over into shaky conflict out of the blue."**

Unfortunate correspondence could likewise seem to be not battling fair. At the point when things get warmed, mates frequently start discussions too cruelly, stall one another, and go to uninvolved animosity.

You don't need to be an expert communicator to redress this issue. A small bunch of abilities can be figured out how to take you from shouting or stalling to talking smoothly and gainfully. Begin by finding something you can identify with or approve in your accomplice. All in all, attempt to see things according to their viewpoint. Maybe you can comprehend how they would be harmed, furious, or baffled by a circumstance — regardless of whether you wouldn't be.

Furthermore, be certain you're truly paying attention to your accomplice, not only trusting that your turn will talk. **"Full focus capacities can help around here, including reflecting back the substance of the conversation to the accessory so they feel appreciated."**

"Assuming that the discussion is excessively extraordinary for accomplices to have regard for one another, then, at that point, a brief break in the discussion is required, so everybody can remain physiologically quiet."

## 2. You Let Untouchables Gain An excessive amount of Impact on Your Marriage

A solid marriage needs an emotionally supportive network of family members and companions — however a few outside connections can apply excessive impact. A parent, companion, or even a kid can hold improper influence over your marriage. "Right when a pariah ends up being excessively connected with a couple's dynamic collaboration, it can provoke battles and decisions that may not agree with the couple's own characteristics and necessities." "The presence of an outsider can disintegrate trust. On the off chance that one accomplice feels like their perspectives and inclinations are reliably superseded, they might lose trust in their life partner's obligation to the relationship."

To shield your marriage from a lot outside impact, limit setting is vital. **"The underlying step is to have straightforward correspondence with your soul mate.**

Examine how you both feel about the association of outsiders and what limits you might want to lay out. Obviously characterize which jobs and limits you need to set as for outsiders."

Then, at that point, convey to the "force to be reckoned with" that your marriage is a two-man just relationship. **"Get a handle on that while you regard their input, a conclusive decisions** concerning your relationship should be made by you and your soul mate."

## 3. You Don't Look for Help for Habit-forming Conduct

Fixation can appear unexpectedly. Other than notable offenders like medications and liquor, exercises like web-based entertainment, work, shopping, betting, and gaming can all become habit-forming.

Anything that the wellspring of fixation, it can split apart you and your accomplice. "At the point when somebody is battling with dependence, their needs frequently shift away from their relationship and friends and family. The substance or conduct of enslavement turns into the focal concentration, leaving less time and profound energy for the relationship." Individuals entangled in fixation may likewise foster clandestine ways of behaving and wind up detaching from their life partner in light of disgrace.

Worn out as it might sound, recognizing a dependence truly is the most important move toward mending — for you as well as your relationship. Whenever you've confessed all to yourself and your companion about what has a hang on you. A prepared specialist can assist you and your mate with exploring recuperation. "This could remember limits for the habit-forming conduct or ramifications for abusing limits … [or] could include care, work out, or taking part in leisure activities."

## 4. You Keep Sex or Actual Love From Your Accomplice

A review distributed in Chronicles of Sexual Conduct observed that a fantastic sexual coexistence and a warm relational environment are both related with conjugal fulfillment.

Likewise, research distributed in April 2023 in Logical Reports uncovered that tender touch was powerfully connected with the level of affection announced between accomplices. Sex and actual closeness are, all things considered, what recognize marriage and heartfelt connections from different connections.

So what befalls marriage when sex and love vacate the premises? Frequently, a sensation of separation creates. A few examinations have shown that lower sexual fulfillment is connected to expanded conjugal issues.

Obviously, bunches of variables can make a longing inconsistency, and sexual recurrence back and forth movements with the rhythms of life, impacted by youngster raising, stress, and actual wellbeing. A time of less sex can be very ordinary. "A disappointing sexual concurrence can make a wedge in the relationship, yet considering the way that there is a fight in this space doesn't be ensured to mean the relationship will be doomed."

Assuming that you're purposefully keeping sex, however, there might be hidden issues dissolving your relationship. "Exactly when it is a consequence of significant distance in the relationship, clients need to manage their more noteworthy picture gives first preceding dealing with sexual closeness." "Similarly, a portion of the time clients have past injury that obstructs their ability to partake in sexual closeness on a more significant level totally."

Her proposal for reviving actual association: Seek a check up in treatment. A specialist can assist you with distinguishing the "why" behind an absence of closeness and move toward reconnecting truly with your mate.

# 5. You're Not in total agreement About Cash

It's OK on the off chance that you and your accomplice make them contrast thoughts regarding cash — yet being on thoroughly contradicting pages about funds overburdens your relationship. Day to day existence involves countless choices about cash, so different monetary methods of reasoning might cause everyday battles.

However, it's generally expected (and, surprisingly, good) for couples to have a few emphatic conversations about cash, a solid relationship is set apart by the manner in which it handles these contentions, says Mill operator. Once more, clear openness is of the utmost importance. **"Couples need to discuss the value and meaning of money in their lives, and what it addresses for them.**

Couples quite often contrast as far as their week by week ways of managing money and can differ or have 'fair quarrels' over those subjects." For however long you're endeavoring to see one another and pursuing split the difference, monetary conflicts don't need to divide you.

## 6. You Let Disregard Creep In, or You Become trapped in a Tough situation

As harmless as disregard could sound, sensations of apathy can be similarly as harming to marriage as super hot resentment. A concentrate in the

Diary of Sex and Conjugal Treatment observed that indifference with regards to a better half was an essential explanation couples entered treatment.

Lack of care can sneak in when you and your mate disregard quality time together, don't share interests, or just become trapped in a tough situation. "While soundness is fundamental, extreme routine can prompt sensations of dreariness and lack of engagement." "External stressors like work, money related issues, or family issues can similarly divert thought and near and dear energy from the marriage."

Long haul unsettled clashes or feelings of hatred can ultimately make profound distance, as well. On the off chance that accomplices don't feel upheld or approved, they might pull out genuinely from the relationship.

To keep the flash alive in your marriage, neutralize lack of care with a touch of fervor. Shock your accomplice sporadically with motions, little gifts, or astonishments. It likewise assists with zeroing in on the things you share practically speaking. "Separate shared targets or errands that you can work on together.

Teaming up on shared targets can reinforce your security." And obviously, routinely speaking with your accomplice about your sentiments, needs, and wants keeps your association solid.

# 7. You Don't Look for Couples' Treatment When You Really want It

Whether your marriage is in desperate waterways or you could simply utilize some calibrating, there's no disgrace in looking for help from a specialist or other psychological wellness proficient. Research shows that couples' advising truly works. A concentrate in the Diary of Conjugal and Family Treatment, for instance, took a gander at 32 couples who partook in sincerely centered couples' treatment, and by and large, couples experienced relationship enhancements two years after treatment. Going to treatment couldn't assist with working on your marriage, it could likewise uncover individual issues that need tending to.

In truth, treatment isn't normally modest, so assuming that you're worried that directing may be a monetary weight, really look at your protection inclusion prior to making a plunge. You could try and contact a nearby spot of love or psychological well-being not-for-profit. Some proposition free or diminished cost advising.

# SAVE YOUR MARRIAGE

Is your relationship not working? Is it safe to say that you are contending or is the fire of your adoration gradually dousing? For what reason is it in some cases so horrendously challenging to keep a relationship decent?

For some individuals in the East, a relationship depends on an organized marriage and in the West on private decision. Both have their great and terrible sides, however in the end everything revolves around ensuring that the relationship develops and you flourish together.

That can be hard. Being seeing someone giving a piece of yourself. You need to consider the other individual. What's more, that is frequently how connections veer off-track. We frequently consider our own perspective and our own prosperity more significant. Our demeanor is additionally part of the way molded by the way of life wherein we live. How would we check our accomplice out? Do you regard the person in question as an equivalent? Deliberately or unknowingly, we frequently don't actually think about our accomplice's sentiments and requirements. Maybe you never discovered that appropriately on the grounds that your folks didn't either or in light of the fact that you needed to miss one or the two guardians from the get-go in your life.

Additionally, men think uniquely in contrast to ladies. Ladies have unexpected feelings in comparison to men and hence respond contrastingly to a similar circumstance. That can prompt numerous errors in a relationship.

# Why do so many relationships get in trouble?

It begins with ourselves. More often than not we contemplate ourselves first. In any event, when you are extremely useful, you might be doing it since it causes you to feel better or on the grounds that you assume you need to.

At the point when either of you thinks about their personal circumstance first, you will become separated. Perhaps one of you is occupied with their prosperity and vocation or with the children. There isn't sufficient consideration left for the accomplice. Or on the other hand one of the two believes they're in an ideal situation with another accomplice and undermines you.

Assuming you offer your accomplice too little consideration and regard, the person will answer by, for instance, becoming far off, lashing out or attempting to reestablish harmony in another manner. In practically no time, profound close to home injuries emerge that can't be recuperated without any problem. The more extended the issues continue, the more those injuries putrefy.

It could likewise be that one of the accomplices has hidden from the other. For instance, a fixation, certain costs or issues. Despite the fact that you might feel that it doesn't irritate the other individual, it will constantly influence the relationship.

## Counteraction is superior to a fix

It begins with being truly mindful that a relationship is considerably more than only for your own pleasure and advantage. Connections are compromise. Frequently we like to take, however we view as giving much harder. You could get a kick out of the chance to give a present or a rose, yet it goes a lot farther than that. To give something that truly sets you back? Is it safe to say that you will surrender a portion of your pride some of the time? To regard the other individual truly?

The way that we primarily ponder ourselves is profoundly imbued in our human qualities. Luckily, there are likewise a lot of instances of genuine romance where the two accomplices truly focus on the other.

Do you have a troublesome relationship and do you believe that your relationship should prosper, then I welcome you to begin finding what is truly significant throughout everyday life. That likewise will significantly affect your relationship.

## Tips for a decent relationship

• Try not to simply consider your own advantage. Deliberately or unknowingly, we frequently predominantly ponder what is great for ourselves. Attempt to imagine the other individual's perspective and find what the person in question likes. Additionally, get some information about this and do whatever it takes not to put your own desires and thoughts first.

• Regard the other. Treat your accomplice in a serious way. Check with yourself to check whether you truly do. On the off chance that your accomplice has an alternate assessment on something, would you say you will consider and regard this assessment?

• It is a cognizant decision to Be seeing someone. Regardless of whether the inclination is now and again less present, it is vital to stay faithful to your decision. In any event, when allurements emerge.

• Try not to be severe towards the other. Despite the fact that the other individual might have done things that hurt you. Attempt to abstain from turning out to be harsh intentionally. Sharpness just makes it harder to get the relationship right once more.

• Accomplish something fun together consistently. By heading off to some place together or accomplishing something fun together, the bond becomes more grounded. Particularly assuming that you're attempting to accomplish something your accomplice truly loves.

• Offer commendations. A commendation is really great for an individual. Search for genuine commendations on your accomplice. Find what inspires the other individual the most. For some these are sweet words, for others time and consideration or a gift, actual touch or support. To figure out more about this, do a quest on the web for the "five dialects of affection".

- Be appreciative. Make a rundown of things in your relationship for which you are or alternately were thankful.

- Tell the truth. A secret mystery can obliterate a relationship. Regardless of whether you believe it's that enormous of an issue. The relationship will continuously experience the ill effects of your mystery.

- Deal with one another. Show up for the other individual when the person in question needs it. At the point when your accomplice is occupied, in torment, or in melancholy.

- Try not to lose yourself. Assuming that you appreciate dealing with your accomplice, remember to deal with yourself as well. Carve out sufficient margin for yourself. Might it be said that you are getting sufficient rest? Likewise examine this with one another.

- Once in a while it takes a ton of tolerance. Your accomplice may not be on a similar profound level as you. It in some cases requires investment and a great deal of discussions to sort out the stuff to draw nearer to one another once more.

- In the event that you have kids, would you say you are a group together? Or then again do you both have various thoughts regarding nurturing? Kids notice this immaculately and exploit it. Ensure that you settle on what rules apply at home and your thought process is significant for the kids. In the event that you disagree with your accomplice's choice, discuss it when the children aren't anywhere near. Assuming you show that you regard one another, the kids will treat you with more regard.

## Consider the possibility that the relationship doesn't work any longer.

There are generally two individuals in a relationship. If one of the two individuals no longer has any desire to put resources into the relationship, eventually the relationship will separate. It can't generally come from one side, despite the fact that there might be times when it appears to be like that. It may be the case that you two are at something else altogether in the relationship.

Rambling with one another, yet additionally listening great can get a halted relationship in the groove again. Obviously, both of you should focus on energy into the relationship. Some of the time it takes a great deal of endurance and tolerance.

Help from an outsider, for instance a relationship specialist, can help you. Yet, mainly, you both put enough in one another. However, be mindful so as not to lounge around and hang tight for the other individual. Gab with one another and attempt to resolve it together. That occasionally requires some investment. Particularly when agony and distress has been developed throughout the long term. Some of the time it can feel like you're pulling a dead pony, however when there is still love, there is trust.

## Assuming there is misuse or savagery

It's an alternate story on the off chance that there is misuse or savagery in a relationship. At the point when your accomplice mishandles you or your kids, it is horrible. That is most certainly never satisfactory in a relationship. You ought to have a solid sense of reassurance and upheld in a relationship. We don't have practical experience in help for these sorts of circumstances, yet we would like to urge you to rapidly look for help! At the lower part of this page you will find various sites where you can go for help. You can likewise reach us through the Talk (if accessible in your country). We are not proficient consideration suppliers, but rather we can offer a listening ear.

## What's straightaway?

Assuming that you might want to find more about yourself and your relationship, we welcome you to investigate internal harmony, harmony and acknowledgment. That is about how you handle your relationship, yet your whole life and future.

In the accompanying article, I need to assist you with figuring out why you are significant. I trust it will assist you with finding the wellspring of affection and why we really structure connections.

Might you want to find more about why your life and your relationship are significant?

# STEP BY STEP INSTRUCTIONS TO TAKE CARE OF MARRIAGE ISSUES

## 1.) Childishness

Assuming I needed to pick two of the most widely recognized marriage issues I have noticed prompting a bigger number of separations than I can count, childishness, would be tied at #1.

The miserable thing about this conjugal issue is, that we are many times scarcely mindful that it's working out. All things considered, assuming they love you, they ought to do 'this and they ought to do 'that' right?

It makes sense to me.

I do indeed.

The issue with that perspective is, life partners will generally neglect to follow the model shown by the connection among Jesus and the congregation. Jesus' relationship with the congregation did not depend on the thing He was getting.

It is basically impossible to avoid having conjugal issues when self-centeredness is tyrannical.

I need to express oppressive since, as defective creatures, we likewise can't evade thinking about the 'self' more than the two 'selfs' in marriage occasionally.

Correspondence in marriage is by a wide margin, the main expertise companions need to have a hitched existence with less conjugal issues.

Yet, might you at any point envision how troublesome marriage correspondence could accompany a narrow minded companion?

Married couples are called to submit to one another's needs and needs commonly.

An accommodation where life partners are commonly dedicated to meeting the genuine adjusted wants of one another.

What's the normal issue with self-centeredness in marriage?

One companion for the most part winds up focusing on their cravings, assumptions or requirements over the other mate.

 Accordingly, the life partner who isn't being focused on will in general feel disliked, irrelevant, or even angry. What's the arrangement?

Remember that marriage isn't exclusively about you, it's about both of you.

One more approach to saying that is, "marriage isn't about me, it's about we."

Jesus' relationship with the congregation is intended to be a natural illustration of a wonderful association, try to duplicate that.

## 2.) Pride

Pride closes a greater number of relationships than passings do.

Pride is tied at #1 for the most widely recognized marriage issue.

In the event that you at any point pondered, "What causes absence of correspondence in marriage," pride is most certainly a top response.

Pride prompts numerous marriage correspondence issues since pride inspires us to fault our life partner, for things we ought to be exclusively faulted for.

Pride causes marriage issues in light of the fact that, regularly, companions won't concede their wrongs.

At the point when we won't concede wrongs sufficiently long, those wrongs go on in our marriage unfixed.

Envision being hitched to a loudly oppressive spouse. Presently envision that mate declining to say, "Please accept my apologies."

Envision the issues you will have in your marriage when you feel that it's consistently your problem for issues in your marriage and seldom the shortcoming of your life partner.

Managing the issue of pride (arrangement): Comprehend that nobody who strolls this world's surface is great.

Everybody has sins they need to deal with. View at your shortcomings as a chance to further develop what your identity is, not a valuable chance to cause you to really regret what your identity is.

Assuming that you are managing an incredibly prideful life partner, put them around gatherings or a local area of individuals that can consider them responsible.

## 3.) Unforgiveness

It's astonishing to me how unforgiving mates can be.

Particularly, when as defective people we continually need grace for our wrongdoings day to day.

As Christians how might you reliably sin against our God and expect pardoning while obstinately holding resentment against your mate?

On the off chance that you're not Christian, you would essentially concur that nobody is great, and hence, everybody will commit errors.

What number of mix-ups have you made against your companion? Here is a superior inquiry.

How often have you rehashed something similar "botch" that you were asking grace for?

"How would I keep unforgiveness from causing marriage issues?" How would you do that basically?

To start with, remember that you continually cause issues in your marriage that your companion needs to pardon you for. Besides, have tolerance.

 It frequently requires investment to improve. It frequently requires investment to improve.

Take it step by step.

Finally, supplicate that God changes your hearts.

Gain proficiency with the abilities important to restrict these normal relationships issues from becoming marriage-finishing issues by understanding this.

# 4.) Cynicism

This occasionally sucks about wedded life, and what makes it hard to have a blissful hitched life.

Managing an extremely bad companion. "For what reason does having a negative life partner cause marriage issues?"

Cynicism establishes a climate that isn't wonderful to be near.

At the point when hitched couples never again appreciate being around one another, the wedded couples become unmarried couples.

The answer for this normal marriage issue: Petition God for your companion. Put them around sure individuals.

It isn't insightful to straightforwardly address their antagonism. It is normally an inward issue that the life partner needs to manage.

# 5.) Refusal

 Nobody likes to hear that their child is revolting!

I don't intend to be horrible.

What I mean about that proclamation is, that we generally don\'t care to hear reality with regards to ourselves.

We rather stick to what encourages us. Forswearing prompts wedded life issues.

There's no rejecting that. Disavowal makes you oblivious to your flaws.

As it were, you can say disavowal is a far off 'cousin' to pride as in there is a visual impairment to one's shortcomings.

At the point when there is that visual impairment, it becomes difficult to chip away at it, prompting your companion languishing.

Dealing with denial(solution): Improving as a companion frequently implies being confronted with regions in your day to day existence where you are not really ideal.

 Figure out how to embrace truth.

# 6.) Instability

Inconveniences in marriage brought about by frailty seldom have to do with our mate.

Normally, that weakness that is giving your marriage issues was brought about by whoever you dated before your mate.

Allow me to figure. You dated somebody that cheated, or lied habitually? That prompted your heart being broken?

What you didn't understand is that you didn't figure out how to completely trust once more.

Hence, you presently project your previous weaknesses in your ongoing marriage. Your dating issue ought not be your hitched issue.

For instance, you have a vehicle, get in the vehicle, begin the vehicle, and drive that vehicle to work five days every week.

If for reasons unknown, you needed to go to chip away at that sixth day, in view of the illumination of proof (vehicle firing up the past 5 days) you have not a great explanation to sensibly accept that your vehicle wouldn't start on that sixth day.

 I express that to say this, you manage frailties causing your marriage issues by understanding that your companion's consistency of character ought to facilitate your uncertainties.

Your past ought not be projected on your companion.

## 7.) Preventiveness

Guarded listening is an unfortunate thing to do to shape in marriage.

Guarded listening is not welcome in a caring marriage. You must have the option to let your life partner know that they are accomplishing something that harms you without them getting guarded.

The difficulties many wedded couples face in marriage are not having the option to impart a shortcoming to their life partner without their mate getting guarded and somebody turning it around on them.

Turning it around on them might incorporate refusing to accept responsibility for the issues at hand', 'playing 'casualty', or giving the quiet treatment.

This large number of models are instances of preventiveness on the grounds that rather than essentially thinking about what your life partner is expressing to you, you promptly go into assault mode.

Keep this from being your conjugal issue (arrangement): When your mate endeavors to converse with you about something that you are fouling up, don't quickly go on assault mode. All things considered, Delay.

 Stop, and consider what you are hearing. Everything that your life partner is saying to you isn't an assault on your whole person. Everything your mate is saying to you is just one thing about you that can turn out to be better.

## 8.) Untrustworthiness

Tragically, cheating occurs in marriage. It sucks, and ideally, with wonderful individuals, it wouldn't work out.

Cheating shouldn't occur, no individual has the right to feel that sort of grievousness.

Notwithstanding, for this article, I need to adopt a disagreeable strategy.

I'm not adopting this strategy essentially to be questionable.

This point of view should be tended to. I will endeavor to guard the individual cheating.

The Book of scriptures clarifies that companions shouldn't abstain from engaging in sexual relations with one another.

Why?

Since then, Satan will entice you with sex.

Stop. Don't reply. Simply look to comprehend.

There is not any justification for cheating, in any case, there are many times reasons individuals cheat that we can sympathize with.

It doesn't make conning right.

It simply makes it more justifiable.

I heard a tale an up about a lady having 5 youngsters and had to surrender her life (profession and instructive pursuits) to be a housewife and bring up her kids.

Luckily, the dad, her better half, was monetarily laid out and could uphold his family effortlessly.

Anyway, what prompted the spouse's cheating?

The spouse worked excessively, wasn't tender, didn't assist with errands in the house, seldom offered help with day to day assignments including the children, and essentially had the discernment that all he needed to do was give monetarily.

The spouse accepted that having his family need for no good reason monetarily was all he needed to do.

 The spouse calmly attempted to get her significant other to feel how overpowered she felt.

The spouse continually communicated to her better half the way that by itself she felt. She persistently and reliably shared how disliked and undesired she felt.

Her better half gave her sentiments no serious thought. Stand by! That is not any justification to swindle. You're correct. By excuse, we characterize it to mean something almost identical to making that "off-base, a right."

No, there is not a good reason.

Yet, there was an explanation. Furthermore, by reason, I want to say "something that makes something happen."

Indeed, she might have recently left her significant other. She might have taken her and her five children and endeavored to begin a day to day existence free of her better half.

It would have been incredibly troublesome, however, it might have been finished.

As defective people, do we generally consider the most noble thing to do?

Or on the other hand do we typically consider managing the aggravation that we are right now feeling with a prompt joy of some kind?

 Married couples cheating isn't OK, yet it works out, sadly, and we really want to talk tackle that conjugal issue by completely tending to that explanation.

Arrangement? That Sacred writing talks clearly enough.

Spouses will not deny wives the fondness she wants from her significant other. Nothing subs for that.

Spouses will not deny husbands their actual closeness.

There is not a viable alternative for that.

Marriage Correspondence Issues

# 9.) Secrecy

Everybody has privileged insights, isn't that so?

Since everybody has privileged insights, is there any good reason why you shouldn't have yours?

Having that mindset prompts marriage issues.

Issues in a marriage are seldom new issues.

Here and there those issues are issues that never have an opportunity to be discussed.

Many individuals think truth closes relationships.

I for one accept that untruths have obliterated much a larger number of relationships than truth has.

Finishing your battles in marriage might be essentially as straightforward as keeping yourself from staying discreet.

All things considered, assuming your activity is something that must be covered up, why commit the demonstration in any case?

Finishing mystery in marriage (arrangement)- It's difficult being weak right?

It's difficult offering confidential to somebody realizing that the mysterious you offer can be utilized against you.

In any case, wedded couples scripturally talking, are one tissue.

That reality alone uncovers a degree of closeness that will be pursued by wedded couples.

We may not at any point completely show up at that objective, but rather we are to travel that way.

 Take it step by step.

Maybe, uncover a new thing to your companion consistently, and both of you discuss it.

Get familiar with the abilities important to restrict these normal relationships issues from becoming marriage-finishing issues by understanding this.

# 10.) Lies

Lies obliterate confidence in a marriage. Lies annihilate relationships.

"It's a tiny bit of untruth," mates say.

However, if that equivalent "little" lie was told to them, they would be offended.

The answer for lying is basic. Remember that, "genuineness is the smartest idea." Trustworthiness doesn't need to put your companion in a terrible mood.

You sure can see your life partner that their breath smells. Or then again, you can say, "darling your breath isn't charming at present."

# 11.) Sex

I don't know about one wedded couple who has at any point had marriage issues in light of the fact that their companion was eager to engage in sexual relations with them.

 Spouses need to be wanted by their wives.

Spouses need to be wanted by their husbands. How would you take care of sexual marriage issues?

Try not to deny each other of feeling alluring. Straightforward, yet, lovely profound. In the event you missed it, ensuring that your mate reliably feels wanted is the arrangement.

# 12.) Vengeance

We believe the one that hurt we should sting as well.

Hitched couples who are centered around retribution as opposed to working on themselves in marriage for one another will not have a blissful marriage life.

What do you do as opposed to seeking retribution? (arrangement)

You supplicate that God eliminates that desire in you.

That's what you understand assuming God practiced vengeance on you, that you would be in damnation.

Say thanks to God for His Beauty that covers our past, present, and future sins.

# 13.) Absence of Consideration

You center around the things you care about.

Somebody who cares very much about wellness invests a ton of energy at the exercise center.

Some who care very much about their vocation invest a ton of energy working.

There is not a remotely good reason for the one you are in association with not definitely standing out and center.

Underestimating your life partner is the way mates frequently lose center around their companion.

Try not to make this a marriage issue you ordinarily face in your marriage.

Arrangement: "give' your companion day to day your full focus, otherwise known as concentration.

# 14.) Absence of Venture:

How precisely would you say you are assisting your marriage with thriving?

Arrangement Make dynamic strides. You can go to marriage meetings. You could peruse a marriage book. You can stand by listening to a marriage digital recording. This multitude of activities show interest in your marriage.

# 15.) Absence of Help

It's simple for wedded couples to help each other when there is a demise of a friend or family member.

It's simple as far as we're concerned as mates to help each other when something awful occurs.

Could we uphold each other every day, with the basic everyday undertakings?

Issues in the marriage frequently happen in light of the fact that one companion feels like they are distant from everyone else in the everyday upkeep of bringing up kids, or family errands.

 Try not to make that an issue in your wedded life. Arrangement Be aware of what your mate goes through on an everyday premise, and be compassionate. Now and again inquiring, "how was your day," is sufficient.

# 16.) Absence of Personal growth

You are noticeably flawed. Nor is your life partner. Furthermore, learn to expect the unexpected. Regardless of whether both of you proceed to be hitched 40 years, you actually won't accomplish flawlessness.

The least you can accomplish for the individual stayed with you for a long time is to attempt to get better consistently, in unmistakable, deliberate ways.

The arrangement is to reliably 'overhaul' yourself for your life partner.

## 17.) Absence of Sympathy

For what reason is it, that when something happens to us, we need to be perceived and identified with?

However, when something happens to other people, we rush to censure.

Once in a while, your life partner doesn't need or need your judgment, counter, or arrangement.

They simply need you to feel what they are going through.

Assuming that they get cut. That is the thought behind sympathy. Being understanding is the manner by which you keep the absence of compassion from being a conjugal issue. (arrangement)

## 18.) Absence of Information

Putting resources into your marriage ought to lead you to be more learned about various parts of your marriage.

Might you want to be a more heartfelt individual in your marriage?

Do you find being heartfelt one of the difficulties you face in marriage?

Extraordinary, you distinguished a typical marriage issue many wedded couples have.

Peruse books that discussion about sentiment. Go to a meeting where the subject is lighting enthusiasm in your marriage.

Arrangement: Continue to figure out how to turn your shortcomings in your marriage, into assets.

# 19.) Quietness

In the event that you hold quiet to forestall yourself back from offering something unpleasant to your mate, then, at that point, amazing. I hail you for your insight and restriction.

Nonetheless, assuming you are the sort of mate to keep quiet since you could do without, or don't have any desire to discuss marriage issues, then, at that point, your quiet is one of the more regrettable types of normal marriage issues.

Arrangement: Realize when to talk, and when to be quiet. Work on fostering a good arrangement.

## 20.) Insolence

Frequently, slight is a conjugal issue since one companion disagrees with how the other life partner thinks or feels about a specific issue in their marriage.

Rather than figuring out how to deal with those distinctions, the life partners decide to affront each other's perspectives.

Who says your view is right, in the first place?

You accept at least for a moment that you're correct, and of course, your companion is off-base then, at that point, continue to put down their perspective.

Arrangement You really want to remember what sort of spouse or wife you want to be. Would you like to be known as a discourteous mate?

 On the off chance that not, figure out how to manage those distinctions in a manner that doesn't naturally show that your companion is not exactly.

Gain proficiency with the abilities important to restrict these normal marriage issues from becoming marriage-finishing issues.

Look at a more arrangement centered approach beneath.

# TENDING TO NORMAL RELATIONSHIP DIFFICULTIES

Each marriage faces its reasonable portion of difficulties.

Notwithstanding, monitoring these normal issues and tending to them proactively can assist couples with beating them and forestall their acceleration into greater issues.

Quite possibly of the most pervasive test in a marriage is ridiculous assumptions.

Many couples go into marriage with assumptions of what their accomplice ought to resemble or how their relationship ought to unfurl.

These ridiculous assumptions can prompt disillusionment and disappointment.

It is fundamental to have transparent discussions about assumptions and work together to figure out some mutual interest.

Monetary issues are one more typical test looked by many wedded couples.

Cash is many times a touchy theme, and conflicts about funds can strain a relationship.

Open and straightforward correspondence about monetary objectives, planning, and it is vital to spend propensities.

It is fundamental for couples to fill in collectively and settle on monetary choices together, taking into account each other's points of view and tracking down compromises that work for the two players.

## Overseeing Ridiculous Assumptions

Ridiculous assumptions can be inconvenient to a marriage.

At the point when we go into a conjugal association, it is fundamental to comprehend that our accomplice is more than a little flawed and will have defects.

Anticipating that our accomplice should meet all our profound, physical, and scholarly necessities can come down on the relationship.

All things being equal, it is essential to acknowledge and value our accomplice for what their identity is, while additionally supporting each other's development and self-improvement.

Besides, overseeing unreasonable assumptions requires compelling correspondence.

It is important to communicate our necessities and wants plainly, while additionally being available to think twice about grasping our accomplice's limits.

Normal registrations and conversations about assumptions can assist with keeping a good overall arrangement in the relationship and forestall errors.

# Defeating Monetary Obstacles in Marriage

Monetary issues can unleash ruin on a marriage on the off chance that not tended to fittingly.

It is essential for couples to foster a strong monetary arrangement and work together towards their monetary objectives.

Here are a few systems to beat monetary obstacles in marriage:

1.     Create a spending plan: Plunk down together and make an exhaustive financial plan that incorporates all pay, costs, and investment funds objectives. This will assist the two accomplices with having an unmistakable comprehension of the monetary circumstance and pursue informed choices.

2.     Communicate transparently about cash: Examining monetary matters straightforwardly and consistently is fundamental. This incorporates speaking the truth about obligations, monetary worries, and objectives. By keeping up with open lines of correspondence, couples can cooperate towards monetary soundness.

3.     Set monetary objectives together: Laying out shared monetary objectives can propel couples to pursue a typical goal. Whether it's

putting something aside for a house, anticipating retirement, or taking care of obligation, having an unmistakable vision can assist with adjusting endeavors and settle on monetary choices more straightforward.

4.      Seek expert assistance if necessary: at times, couples might find it gainful to look for the direction of a monetary guide or instructor. These experts can give master exhortation and assist with exploring complex monetary circumstances.

Keep in mind, conquering monetary obstacles requires persistence, understanding, and cooperation.

By cooperating, couples can defeat monetary difficulties and construct a more grounded starting point for their marriage.

# Keys to a Cheerful Marriage

A blissful marriage is based on an underpinning of affection, trust, and common regard.

While each relationship is novel, there are sure key components that add to conjugal satisfaction.

We should investigate a portion of these keys to a cheerful marriage:

1. Effective correspondence: Correspondence is the foundation of any fruitful relationship. It includes offering one's viewpoints and sentiments as well as effectively paying attention to one's accomplice. Great correspondence takes into account grasping, split the difference, and the goal of struggles.

2. Physical closeness: Actual closeness assumes an essential part in a cheerful marriage. It is a way for couples to interface genuinely and truly, reinforcing their bond. Communicating love through actual touch, motions, and closeness helps cultivate a profound feeling of association and closeness.

3. Quality time together: Hanging out is fundamental for keeping a cheerful marriage. It permits couples to support their relationship, make shared recollections, and reinforce their profound association. Whether it's date evenings, end of the week excursions, or essentially

appreciating each other's conversation at home, cutting out devoted time for one another is urgent.

4. Healthy correspondence: Sound correspondence includes communicating positive feelings as well as successfully tending to clashes and conflicts. It is essential to resolve issues as they emerge, as opposed to allowing them to putrefy and make hatred. This should be possible by rehearsing undivided attention, sympathy, and tracking down commonly pleasing arrangements.

# Flourishing in Wedded Life

Flourishing in wedded life requires devotion, exertion, and a readiness to adjust and become together.

Here are a few techniques that can assist couples with flourishing in their wedded life:

1. Appreciating the easily overlooked details: Little tokens of adoration and appreciation can go quite far in sustaining a relationship. Basic behaves like saying "thank you," leaving a sweet

note, or astounding your join forces with their number one treat can have a massive effect.

2. Balancing online entertainment: In the present computerized age, finding some kind of harmony between investing quality energy with your accomplice and taking part in virtual entertainment is significant. Defining limits and assigning gadget spare energy can assist with making a more profound association and forestall sensations of disregard.

3. Seeking expert assistance: Assuming correspondence issues, closeness issues, or other relationship issues continue to happen, looking for proficient assistance can be useful. Marriage mentors or advisors can give direction and backing to assist couples with exploring through troublesome times and fortifying their relationship.

4. Celebrating achievements: Praising achievements, both of all shapes and sizes, is a superb method for keeping the flash alive in a marriage. Whether it's a wedding

commemoration, an advancement at work, or an individual accomplishment, recognizing and praising these achievements together can create a feeling of bliss and shared achievement.

All in all, marriage issues are a characteristic piece of each and every relationship, except they can be overwhelmed with persistence, understanding, and difficult work.

By keeping up with open lines of correspondence, overseeing assumptions, resolving monetary issues, and sustaining the profound association, couples can explore through the difficulties and fabricate a blissful and satisfying wedded life.

Keep in mind, an effective marriage is a nonstop excursion of development and disclosure.

Embrace the challenges and commend the delights, knowing that with responsibility and love, you can conquer any impediment that comes your direction.

# 16 MOST NORMAL MARRIAGE ISSUES THAT LEAD TO SEPARATION

Individuals have this freshly discovered view on marriage, where that's what they trust on the off chance that it's somewhat flawed you ought to simply call it quits. Truly, no marriage is great. A marriage requires two gatherings who love each sufficiently other to take the necessary steps to make their marriage last. There will be a great deal of normal marriage issues that emerge during your lifetime. Together, you can deal with them, and keep on building an enduring relationship.

## 1. Unfaithfulness

Cheating is #1 on my rundown tragically, in light of the fact that it is one of the most widely recognized marriage issues. Ongoing treachery measurements show that in 33% of relationships, possibly one or the two accomplices confess to cheating. That is one out of three!

Treachery doesn't be guaranteed to need to mean engaging in sexual relations with somebody outside your marriage. It can likewise mean having sexual longings for somebody or even sincerely trusting in somebody with the craving of having a relationship with them. Certain individuals additionally consider watching erotic entertainment as cheating-ensure you and your companion are in total agreement about this!

Nobody goes into their marriage with the expectation of betraying their life partner. The most widely recognized purposes behind individuals being faithless are vengeance, and sexual or potentially close to home disappointments.

To Keep away from Disloyalty:

Focus on correspondence with your accomplice. Tell them you needing. Assuming that you want more closeness, attempt to track down ways of getting your accomplice in total agreement. Assuming you really want daily encouragement, have a go at moving toward your companion with practically no displeasure in your voice, that will get the discussion going gravely, and you won't ever make yourself clear.

Try not to set yourself in that frame of mind to swindle. Try not to be companions with the other gender while your marriage is rough. Try not to trust in the other gender about your relationship. On the off chance that you wind up fostering an improper relationship with somebody, tell your mate before it goes crazy. The grass isn't greener on the opposite side — It's greener where you water it!

## 2. Compulsion

Being dependent on something will go on and on forever well. Your marriage should be your main need throughout everyday life, number one! At the point when you're dependent on something it will in general be the need. You must kick any dependence on have to the check!

There are so many things that individuals can be dependent on. There are more normal things like medications, liquor, porn, and betting. Yet, there additionally different things you could be dependent too without absolutely acknowledging it, for example, sex, burning through cash, computer games, thus some more.

Flame resistant is the BEST film ever for couples who are feeling far off a result of one's fixation! It's a marriage saver!

**To Keep away from Enslavement:**

Try not to permit yourself to be enticed. Assuming you're attempting to stop drinking liquor, don't go out with individuals who drink, ask your accomplice not to drink before you, and keep away from liquor no matter what. It's truly difficult to dispose of a fixation when you're encircled by it.

Find support on the off chance that you really want it. Go to bunch treatment, read books, keep a diary. Effectively consider yourself responsible. Tell individuals you're stopping, they can likewise consider you responsible!

# 3. Various Perspectives on Significant Things

There are a few things that ought to be examined before marriage. These remember perspectives for cash, religion, values and ethics, having kids, housework, occupations, and the rundown goes on! You must be in total agreement with your life partner about specific things, or your marriage will be a battle all along

**To Try not to Have Various Perspectives:**

Preferably, significant things ought to be examined before marriage, however that doesn't necessarily in all cases occur, and here and there things change. All things considered, you Should think twice about. You both should consent to a fair compromise before one of the issues makes your marriage self-combust!

# 4. Poisonous Individuals

There will constantly be individuals in your day to day existence that are totally harmful to your marriage. These can incorporate companions of a similar sex, or the other gender, relatives and parents in law, and ex-accomplices. Anybody who rushes to advise you to leave, or discusses your accomplice, or energizes unfaithfulness, or whatever other improper way of behaving that will be terrible for your marriage isn't somebody you need in your life.

**To Stay away from Poisonous Individuals:**

Ditch them pronto. One of the fundamental issues relationships face is that every individual is trusting in another person about the issues in their marriage when they ought to be let their life partner know how they feel. Converse with your mate! Assuming you believe you really want to advance it out beyond time just to quiet down first, get it on paper! You will be astounded how much this can help.

# 5. Misuse

Physical, verbal, and psychological mistreatment are normal issues that a many individuals are looking in their marriage. Misuse ought to never be endured. It's a certain fire method for obliterating any relationship. A many individuals, all kinds of people have no clue they are survivors of misuse. Verbal and psychological mistreatment incorporate ridiculing, shouting, dangers and terrorizing, segregating/disregarding, embarrassing, thus considerably more.

To Keep away from Misuse:

Clarify that the maltreatment won't go on without serious consequences, and if your life partner needs to stay wedded to you they need to look for help to control themselves. Assist them with tracking down outlets to alleviate their pressure, seek them into help, keep away from triggers. Show them that you support them in their excursion to personal growth.

# 6. Online Entertainment

Virtual entertainment ruins connections in such countless ways. In the first place, it makes individuals have ridiculous assumptions. Individuals just post about the positive qualities in their day to day existence, so you see this large number of others with their "awesome" relationship, house, monetary circumstance, and so on. Nobody is great, whether your companions on Facebook appear to be.

It additionally gives people the possibility that assuming that they post online about their affection for their companion, that it's similarly on par with confronting them about that directly. It's not. Tell your mate how you feel directly. Get things done to show them the amount they mean to you. Talk is cheap.

Web-based entertainment is a favorable place for hunters. Individuals love show, and they are following your page only searching for the humblest touch of something your family could be battling with so they can utilize it against you.

To Keep away from Web-based Entertainment Obstructing Your Marriage:

Try not to fixate on what you see on the web. It's not reality. Try not to post about issues you're having in your relationship. Try not to trust in somebody over the web. Online entertainment can be great, you can interface with far off family, or use it for your business, however assuming no good thing is emerging from your virtual entertainment, and it creates an excessive number of issues inside your marriage, simply dispose of it.

# 7. Absence of Correspondence

Openness is of the utmost importance. Did you have at least some idea that unfortunate correspondence is the number 1 justification for separation? Over disloyalty and absence of adoration... unfortunate correspondence is on the first spot on the list of most normal marriage issues! Individuals accept that their companion ought to simply understand what they need, and what they're thinking. It doesn't work that way.

On the off chance that you need something done a specific way, or you are unglued about something, you should impart your requirements to your accomplice. Anticipating what they should figure is upsetting to them since they don't see what you need, and distressing on you since you're not getting anything it is you want.

**To Stay Away from Absence of Correspondence:**

Go to your life partner first, about everything! Periodically, all somebody needs is to vent and let everything out. Whenever you've done that you can begin with a new demeanor. Try not to go let all that out on a companion, or a collaborator, let it out on your life partner. They must show up for you. Ensure you are in total agreement about everything. Explain that you are in agreement regardless.

# 8. Youngsters

This one is intense. Youngsters can bring a wedded couple nearer than at any other time.

You cooperated to make a daily existence. You presently have a more profound association than you ever have previously. Be that as it may, youngsters can likewise overwhelm your marriage.

Your marriage used to be your principal need, and presently your obligations have moved, and youngsters are the fundamental concentration. You have a consistent sensation of overpower, you're close to home, and a ton of your pressure will in general get taken out on your companion.

## To Keep away from Kids Overburdening Your Marriage:

Continue to date your life partner. Try constantly to intrigue them. Accomplish something decent for them regular. Continuously focus on night out on the town. Attempt to level out the responsibility, between diaper changes, and errands, and other obligation. Regardless of whether your companion isn't investing a similar measure of effort, continue to do the best that you can with it. You never realize exactly how much pressure an individual is under. Continue to treat your accomplice the manner in which you need to be dealt with, and ultimately it will click for themselves and they will actually want to respond all of the adoration you have given to them.

# 9. Deceitfulness

Nothing ruins a marriage quicker than contemptibility. Trust is so difficult to recapture whenever it has been broken. Indeed, even with the littlest untruth, it will create some issues inside your relationship. Whenever you've lied, you simply continue onward. You need to mislead conceal your untruths, etc.

Whether you're lying about your past, or your acts of unfaithfulness, or cash, or your convictions, anything it could be... reality will liberate you.

**To Stay away from Deceitfulness:**

Confess all quickly. Try not to progress forward with a falsehood. Conceding reality can be truly challenging, however it is a lot more straightforward to regard somebody who takes ownership of their errors, than somebody who keeps on lying. Make it a highlight tell every bit of relevant information, starting now and into the foreseeable future.

# 10. Closeness Issues

Sex is an immense piece of marriage. Getting physically involved with somebody has an approach to bringing both of you closer, and laying out a more profound association with each other. Normally, individuals have various longings in the room. Anything that those wants might be, you and your mate must be in total agreement.

**To Try not to Have Closeness Issues:**

Focus on sex. Regardless of whether you believe you want it frequently, your accomplice may. Sex can bring you two nearer together the two actually and inwardly. Impart what it is that you need. Be receptive to your companion's longings. In the event that there is something you two can't settle on, attempt to figure out a fair compromise.

Without settling, a marriage won't stand the test of time.

# 11. Self-centeredness

It is normal to understand what you need and to focus on it for things to be the manner in which you need them. However, while you're placing your requirements over your companions, and your not able to think twice about... being egotistical.

It's difficult to understand that you are being egotistical here and there. As far as some might be concerned, it's simply the manner in which they've forever been. It's a propensity, a hard one to break! Whether you're being childish with your time, or your cash, or whatever else, it needs to stop.

**To Keep away from Self-centeredness:**

Do the specific inverse. You should be sacrificial with regards to your accomplice. You want to place their necessities over your own. Focus on them in your day to day existence. Does this mean you indulge them so they don't need to do anything for themselves? No, on the grounds that they will take on a similar caring demeanor. They will focus on you, and they will place your requirements over their own. You deal with them, and they will deal with you.

## 12. Private matters

You can't cherish somebody until you figure out how to adore yourself. Indeed, you can have love for somebody... yet you can't cherish them the correct way! Whether you generally disapprove of envy, self-mischief, or even dysfunctional behavior like gloom or nervousness, and so forth, having such issues overwhelms your marriage.

It's difficult to have an inspirational perspective when your head is loaded up with negative considerations about yourself. It's unfavorable to your marriage in the event that you, at the end of the day, are a ticking delayed bomb.

**To Stay away from Private matters Influencing Your Marriage:**

Figure out how to deal with it. Have a go at journaling, exercise, guiding, and let your accomplice in on what you want from them. On the off chance that you have, or figure you could have a psychological sickness, make a point to talk with your PCP to look for legitimate therapy.

## 13. Not Hanging out

It's challenging to keep a relationship on favorable terms when you don't hang out. Without being together, you cut out closeness, date evenings, and great correspondence. Whether you're investing the majority of your energy in work, or leisure activities, or something different... your marriage must be really important.

**To Stay away from Not Getting to know one another:**

Put night out on the schedule, and get it going. Make it a highlight enjoy x measure of evenings at home with your companion. Assuming work consumes you, attempt to include your life partner, check whether they can help you.

Attempt to find leisure activities you can do together.

## 14. Holding Hard feelings

Holding resentment resembles beginning a fierce blaze. It's ceaseless. On the off chance that you are holding something against your mate, it will cause all that you to do transform into a battle. On the off chance that your mate is as yet accomplishing something they shouldn't that is a certain something, however assuming that they have recognized that they've committed an error, and they are giving their best for move past it, you can not hold resentment.

To Try not to Hold Hard feelings:

You need to figure out how to move past it. Whether it be through guiding, or journaling, or talking it through in a sound way with your mate, you must track down a way! Try not to allow those negative contemplations to consume your life. Center around the positive.

## 15. Pursuing for 50/50

Everybody says that two individuals need to invest a similar measure of energy into their relationship-50/50. Wrong! You should do the best that you can with it, 100 percent. A relationship isn't tied in with keeping track of who's winning, you don't attempt to match how much exertion your life partner is giving. You do everything you can consistently! In some cases, your very best won't be a lot. Everybody has their terrible days. Be that as it may, in the event that your accomplice is doing their absolute best, they will be there to bring you up.

**To Try not to Go after 50/50:**

Try not to keep track of who's winning. Try not to put forth how much attempt you're placing in depending on how much your companion is giving. You set forth the greatest energy, and your companion will do likewise. It's difficult to battle with somebody who simply tries constantly to give their all.

# 16. Affront

I saved this one for last since this whole rundown could fit under this classification. In the event that you don't have regard your mate, you will not have an enduring marriage. Showing insolence to somebody is the quickest method for losing them from your life.

Irreverence can be depicted in such countless ways. Not caring much about them, loudly mishandling them, cheating, being deceptive, overlooking them, underestimating their viewpoints... and so on. It causes extreme displeasure when somebody has such an absence of regard, that you're suppositions appear to be unimportant, and your presence feels undesirable.

# CONCLUSION

Speak with your life partner on the off chance that there is anything you don't regard about them. Work through it, and continue on from it. Individuals can't fix what they don't know is. Get to know your companion, so you can see all that there is to regard. Notice how focused, patient, capable, brilliant, committed, fair, or even the way that caring your mate is. Anything it very well might be, center around their separate highlights.

Marriage is about collaboration, a decent spouse makes a decent wife. There is no such thing as an ideal marriage, so don't let these normal marriage issues hold your relationship back from flourishing. However long you commit to never abandon your companion, and take the necessary steps to make things work, you are getting everything done as needs be. Also, that adoration is infectious. Allow it to spread.

www.ingramcontent.com/pod-product-compliance
Lightning Source LLC
Chambersburg PA
CBHW071608270726

48661CB00019B/1655